Left Across the Border

Teenage Depression Series Book 1

by

Patrice M Foster

Patricemfoster.com

Left Across the Border
Copyright © 2016 Patrice M. Foster
ISBN: 978-0998187433
Library of Congress Control Number: 2016917887
Cover design by http://yocladesigns.com

Table of Contents

Introduction

Sadness and depression are not the same things. In this series of books on teens and depression, we'll take a long, hard look at how easy it can be for a teen to believe they just feel sad when they are actually depressed. Many people, including teens, senior citizens and adults do not always recognize they are suffering from depression. After all, as one source says, "Depression is different from regular sadness because it lasts longer and affects more than just a person's mood."

Sometimes, people don't see or realize that sadness has lasted for so long and has become so large that it cannot be as simple as feeling a bit blue or sad. It may have even taken over the person's entire life, leaving them tired, achy, and unable to enjoy any part of life.

Unfortunately, there are always things that cause depression, and this may be why a teen thinks that it is "only" sadness. They might move far away from home, have their heart broken by a boyfriend or girlfriend, experience bullying at school, or feel the emotional impact of discrimination. Because modern teens are also more connected due to social media, they may not get any sort of break from the issues leading to depression.

We read headlines of bullying that goes on during school hours and just continues all night on sites like Facebook or through endless text messaging. This can make it easy for a teen to become depressed, and have no way of escaping it.

RECOGNIZING DEPRESSION

Because it can be hard for a depressed teen to know what is happening, it is important for them or their loved ones to know the signs of depression. They include:

- Negative thinking - Depression makes it hard to think clearly. Thoughts like, "Nothing will ever be better," or "This is too hard for me to deal with," are very common. This is why a depressed teen believes they are worthless, that life is not worth living, or that no one loves them - even though this is not true at all.
- Tired or without energy - A depressed teen often sleeps a lot, feels very tired, and may not move that much. Just doing things like bathing, changing clothes, or going out to the store may feel too exhausting. It also makes it hard for them to think or

pay attention, and many depressed teens say they cannot focus on school or even conversations.

- Negative mood or feelings - Depression is not only feeling sad. Someone who is depressed may be angry, annoyed, or feeling isolated. The negative mood or feelings are not brief, but ongoing for weeks or longer. This is why the person who is depressed may feel defeated, alone, helpless and even exhausted.
- Withdrawing - Most depressed people will pull away from their friends, families, and activities that they once loved. This only makes them feel more isolated, and makes it even harder to think clearly about their situation.
- Physical signs - In addition to being tired, people with depression will tend to gain or lose weight because they do not move or eat enough. They might have headaches or sleep too much or not enough.

That is a lot to take in, but if you or someone you know is showing any of these symptoms, they might be depressed. Sadly, a lot of teens with depression also have other signs that they hide. Some people cut themselves. Some people have eating disorders, and some may start using drugs or alcohol to "escape" the pain they feel.

GETTING HELP

No matter how bad depression might be, there is always help. Doctors are a good first step as they can do a checkup on the person to make sure their bodies are okay, and then they can help them find the type of counselor or therapist they will need to overcome depression.

While many people don't want to work with a counselor, it is important to remember that therapists and counselors will help them to understand all of the emotions and feelings they are struggling with. They will help to break negative thinking and feelings, and they help the depressed person improve their self-esteem and begin to overcome the struggle.

Depression is caused by many things, and even if the problems that trigger the depression cannot be ended (bullies, discrimination, relationships, and so on), the person who feels depressed can learn how to overcome it. They can learn about self-care, self-esteem, and how to see things in a healthier way. Their counselor, family, or friends can also help them to remember or rediscover themselves, and this is a big part of beating depression for good.

Depression is no joke, and if it is ignored, it can have horrible consequences. Teens, adults, and even seniors who do not get help with their depression may end up harming themselves or even ending their own lives.

FINDING SOLUTIONS, SHARING STORIES

There are answers, and often we can find them when we read about others who are brave enough to share their stories of depression.

In the story that follows, we hear about a young immigrant girl who bravely travels to the United States in hopes of a better life. Believing that her family will soon

follow, the young girl instead encounters many problems. Alone and miserable, she slides into deep depression. Because she has no friends and does not speak English well, she remains depressed, and as things get worse, she begins harming herself as a form of emotional escape.

Dealing with bullying, sexual abuse, poverty, isolation, and neglect, she just falls deeper into depression and believes that she has no one who can help her or who cares. She goes beyond just harming herself and decides to take her life. Fortunately, she does not succeed.

It is just when things cannot get any worse that she finds herself in the hands of mental healthcare experts who help her begin to heal. These experts, along with the girl's new foster family, show her that she is not alone, and that life is always worth living.

It is a hard story to hear, and one that shows how easy it can be to think to yourself, "Well, I am just too sad and I cannot bear it any longer." It is a tale that shows how easily it can be to feel worthless, unlovable, and without any hope at all. Most importantly, it shows how depression can make you begin to truly believe all of these things, and how depression can make you too tired and too defeated to even fight to save yourself.

Anyone who reads this story will learn something about depression, but even more importantly, they will see how to overcome it. It is possible to beat depression, but as this teen's story shows, you need to accept help and work hard to understand what caused you to become so depressed. In the end, you must realize that no one is alone and that there is help out there.

Chapter One

LEAVING HOME

There is a saying about eyes and how they can be like a window into your soul. I guess that's probably true.

Look into my eyes. Well, you can try, but most of the time I won't really let you. If you do see into my eyes, I think you would see my soul. You would see that there is brightness and there is darkness because my soul has both.

My soul is bright because I grew up with two parents who love me and two sisters that I love to the moon and back. That gives me something like a bright star that shines inside of me, and that star will never go out. Mine shines, and you can see it in my eyes.

You can also see that there is darkness in my eyes, and I think it is the hole that was made in my soul when I left home and left my family behind.

My name is Flora, and I am originally from Mexico. My story is not what you might expect when you look at me, though. I am usually nicely dressed and clean, but I am not what you would call "complete."

There is a big part of me that I left across the border, and that is one of the reasons there is sadness in my eyes and my soul. The emptiness I feel is most of it, but there is a lot of sadness because of what happened from the moment I left home until a long time later.

First, let me tell you about leaving home, and then the sad story that followed.

CROSSING OVER

I won't tell you a lot about my crossing into America from Mexico. Why? It is difficult to describe what it is like.

Now that I know the words and my English is better, I have to tell you that the journey was hot, bleak, glaring, and bright. It was also dark, quiet, and scary. The land is open and dry. We saw snakes and poisonous spiders, coyotes, and lots of dried up trees and dirt. Sometimes, we found big jugs of water left in secret and hidden places just for people like us, sneaking into the United States.

We were in a group, and they were all strangers to me. We all spoke Spanish, but we didn't really talk much. We were too tired and scared to ever say anything. There were older men, little babies, other kids, and women.

We knew that we were all "illegals", making our way to a better life.

That's something I wish people could understand better about the illegals from Mexico who cross over to the United States. Most of us are not doing it because we want something for nothing. I didn't leave my parents and sisters because I wanted an easy life. How could leaving my whole family be easier?

I wasn't looking for lots of money, food, fancy clothes, or a big house. We just wanted to stop being so poor.

"Flora can go," said Papa one night, "And then we can follow her a bit later."

I told myself that I could be like the hero of a story, making the path so they could follow. Only, it didn't work out like that.

My parents work hard, but we have always struggled, and it was almost impossible for them to save the money they needed to get me across the border.

"Jorge can get Flora a green card and even across the border," Papa said. And I believed that trusting the smuggler named Jorge was the right way to do things. The green card was important because it would be a way that would allow my family to come over, legally, later.

We all worked hard to save up and to pay Jorge the money he wanted so he would take me across. It was something we all agreed to so that our whole family could have a better and safer life, not any of the other things I hear people accuse immigrants of wanting. I didn't think about going to a dentist or a doctor for free or getting free food or free housing. I just wanted to find a way to work, earn money, and bring my family together again.

Sorry, I am jumping ahead. I want to tell you a bit more about crossing so that you can understand why it is such a hard and sad thing to live through.

MAKING OUR PLANS

When my family talked about it, we thought about the many train riders who take the freight trains north towards the border. We thought about the danger of crossing the Rio Grande. We worried about the journey. Then we learned it would be from Mexico into Southern California, and that meant we'd cross the desert.

"Oh Lord," Mama said, "The desert...I don't know if Flora is strong enough." And she started to cry.

"We can prepare her properly," Papa said, but he didn't look happy.

I won't lie; I was very scared of that, but I knew that I had to be brave. After all, I was the hero of the story!

We met where Jorge told my parents to be, and we were told that I could not bring a lot of things except the clothes I was wearing. I wore a few layers, and I also tucked some important things into my clothes too.

My precious belongings included a picture, my sisters, Camila and Mia had given me that day.

"It is our family," little Mia said, and held up the picture of four stick figures in a house and two (grandma and grandpa) in another house nearby.

"This is the phone number for Mateo," Papa said as he tucked the slip of paper into my small purse, "He's...he's like family and will have a room for you. Call him when you are safely across."

I also had a little money that I would use to find Mateo and settle in.

When we gathered to leave, I thought I would break in two; it hurt so much to say goodbye. I cried and held my father. He hugged me so hard, and I could feel that he did not want to let me go.

"Be a brave girl, Flora," Mama choked out over her sobs.

I could barely understand her; she was so emotional. My sisters gave me kisses, and we all said we would see each other again soon.

We repeated it over and over. "Soon, Mama, soon, soon, soon..."

ON THE WAY

I like the word "bleak" to describe the journey. Bleak means miserable and unfriendly, and that was exactly what our group and our journey were, miserable and unfriendly.

I made friends with two girls, Luciana and Ximena, but they were not really nice, just the same age as me. Luciana told me that she had to leave home because a guy from a local gang had said he "liked" her, and it could mean he might just take her from her family.

"They share their girlfriends," she whispered to me, "And that means I would have had to have sex with everyone in the gang."

"I heard the same things," Ximena said, "But where I am from, if a guy liked you it could mean he just wanted to rape you, and a lot of girls disappear after that."

I didn't like to hear them talk like that. I was not a girl who was having sex with boys or men, and these two spoke about it like it was the normal thing to do at our age. I was too embarrassed to tell them that I had not had sex or even kissed a boy!

After that, I thought that being poor was not so horrible if that is what those girls had to live with. I could understand why they would escape to America if they could not feel safe in their own bed at home.

I don't know if I could have left my sisters behind if I thought something like that could ever happen. I know it sounds weird, but it made me feel better to be making the journey if it could mean that I might save my little sisters from something so awful.

When you are crossing a border, you don't have a lot of time to talk or even think. There is so much to worry about. At night, things were very bad. Some of the older men began to tell us girls that we should lie next to them to be safe. My two friends told me to be careful, and to stay with them.

"Listen," Ximena whispered, "I can teach you stuff that will keep a dirty old man away!"

Luciana laughed and said, "I have a few tricks too!" And then showed us her knife.

I wasn't sure what to think about it, but I was so tired that it was hard even to care. Later, I would remember this and wish I had let them teach me their tricks.

And then, when the days all got blended together, and just as I thought I would die from the heat and being so tired, we were suddenly approaching a fence. We waited for the sun to set, and made our way through the fence. We had a short walk after that, and then we were racing to a van that was waiting for us. That was it…we had made it.

Chapter Two

IN AMERICA

I realized that our group was going to split up right away. I got the green card that I was supposed to get from Jorge, and I asked what I was supposed to do next.

"Call the people your father told you to call," he said and pointed to a pay phone."Your green card is because of them."

So, I used the money I had to call the number that my papa gave me, and Mateo came to pick me up.

"We are not your family," Mateo said, and gave me an ugly look, "Not even close. Your papa was wrong to lie about that. I agreed to take you for the money and to get you a green card."

I felt sad that my father had lied to me.

When I got to the house, I was surprised that so many people lived there. I was sharing a bedroom with four other people, and there were 15 of us in the small house. I made friends with one of the other girls, who was a little older than me. She had dark hair and wore nice clothes.

"Hi," she said, "my name is Sofia."

She smiled and took my hand and brought me inside to our room.

"I know it seems crowded," she said as I looked around, "But I've been here almost a year and it is okay, and when you start school you will hardly be here at all. And when you are home you'll be busy helping out."

It sounded a lot like being back at home, and I started to feel a bit better.

Later that night I was able to clean myself with a bit of warm water, and there was some food for us to eat. I began to think that everything would be okay, but I worried about my clothes.

I kept the layers on even when it was so hot in the desert, but I still had just two pairs of underwear, two shirts, and one pair of pants. The trip almost ruined my shoes, but I didn't have any money for new ones.

I was daydreaming about going to an American school as I began to fall asleep, but then I felt my bed move like someone was climbing onto it. I turned to look, and it was one of the men, Samuel, from the other bedroom across the hall.

"Get out of my bed," I said to him and tried to kick him, but he leaped forward and slammed his palm over my mouth and squeezed my face. He leaned in close, and he smelt like sweat and cigarettes and old food.

"All you girls let me in your bed," he whispered in my ear as he seemed to crush me.

I didn't understand what he meant. Why did Sofia not tell me about this? I began to fight with him, but he just squeezed my face harder and said, "If you don't just shut up, you will be sorry."

I don't want to explain what he did next. I tried to fight. I tried not to think about what he was doing. I knew then why those other girls had run away from home and made the journey away from Mexico. I wished I had let them show me their tricks for making dirty old men leave them alone.

I finally understood what they were talking about when they said that some of the men who liked them just wanted to hurt them. Samuel did terrible things, hurting me, and making me feel all wrong.

I didn't sleep at all, and when he left, I went to wake up Sofia and tell her about it.

"You have to learn to ignore him," she said, "If you cause trouble here they are going to find a way to send you back."

I won't lie to you. I thought about going home right then. That's all I wanted was to go home to my family. I told her that too. "Fine," I said, "I'll tell everyone that I want to go home."

She smiled at me and said, "They will tell your parents what has happened, and then your parents will never be able to be proud of you." She was looking hard into my eyes when she said it. "What would your parents say if they knew what you let him do to you? What would they say after they spent all of that money to bring you here?"

I was so angry and so sad all at the same time. "I didn't let that filthy, smelly Samuel touch me," I argued, "He was hurting me, and he did things that my father would kill him for doing."

"But your father is far, far away," she said, "And you are all alone. If you fight with Samuel, he might hurt you more, and he might also make sure you get kicked out of the house."

I sat outside that morning, hiding from everyone, and trying to think. What should I do? I did not speak any English yet. I was not old enough to be alone, and I didn't have any money.

I took out the picture my sister had drawn for me and talked to it just like I was talking to my family. "What should I do, Mama? Papa?" I was hoping that I would hear them giving me advice. Then, I did hear my mother. I remembered her telling me to be brave, and kissing me goodbye.

"I will be as brave as I can, Mama," I whispered, "I will go to school, learn English and try to make things better, so I can get away from Samuel and this horrible house. I will go to school and get a job, and then you can come, and it will all be better."

GOING TO SCHOOL

I was able to get into school because I had the green card. The problem was that I had no English at all. When I went to school, it was so confusing, and I felt lost all of the time. The way some of the kids looked at me; I could see that they didn't like me.

They were saying things to me that I didn't understand, but I could see in their eyes and their faces that they were calling me names. One of the boys pinched his nose and waved his hand in front of his face, and I saw that he was trying to tell me that I smelled.

I remember once, before coming to the United States, that I had been happy and excited by the idea of going to an American school. The things that happened when I arrived, though, were making it really hard to think about anything at all. I was never happy, and I began to believe that I would never be happy again.

"What's wrong with you, Flora?" I angrily asked myself, "You should be glad and smiling because your dream of going to school, learning English, and getting closer to bringing your family to the United States was all starting."

I couldn't feel happy about it. All I could think about was how bad Samuel made me feel when he had touched me and done things to my body, how dirty and smelly everything was in the house, and how miserable I felt. I couldn't read signs on the streets. I didn't understand what people in the grocery store said when I went to help with the shopping, and I didn't always know what was in the cans or boxes of food because I couldn't read the English labels.

Today, I know that I was suffering a lot because of the isolation.

I really was all alone in my struggles. Not only was Samuel abusing me, but I was unable to wear clean clothes, clean my body properly, or tell anyone about it. I lived in fear of being kicked out and sent home, and I had no one to help me.

IT GETS WORSE

I was 14 when I left home, and I knew some things about my body. I knew from my Mama that I would start to grow hair, that my breasts would get bigger, and that I would start to bleed. She explained all of these things to me, but I was embarrassed and tried to make her stop talking.

"Mama," I remember whining, "Stoooppp…"

She laughed at me and hugged me and said, "Oh, Flora, you are such a sweet little girl. Someday, though, you will grow up, and

I don't want you to feel ashamed or embarrassed. It is okay."

I am lucky that Mama kept repeating things to me to be sure I understood them. I think she knew I would be on my own when these things happened, and she wanted to be sure that I wasn't too scared by it all. When these things did start, I really wanted Mama, but then I remembered how she had already explained so many of them to me, and I remembered what to do.

She explained it was puberty, that it was natural, and that it would mean I was growing up. When I first learned this from her, I was unhappy. I did not want to grow up and be an adult. When it happened, though, and I was all alone in the world, it was comforting because I felt like a grown up.

It was not easy, because I missed Mama and my family. It was also not easy because my house was crazy. Everyone lived for themselves. No one really shared things. No one really helped anyone else. Sometimes there was no hot water left, and so I had to wash in cold water, and because I had only one school outfit, kids began to pick on me.

I look back now, and I can see just why I was so sad all of the time. I was dirty because we had no shampoo, only dish soap. I washed myself, my hair, and my clothes in the cheap soap. My body was changing, so I was growing hair, and I started to have what one of the meaner girls at school called "BO." She meant that I smelled bad, but it was because I could not buy things like deodorant.

My English was getting better, but that didn't help because I started to finally understand the mean names the kids called me. They told me I smelled like a fart. They said I was a "wetback," but I never knew what that meant except that I was Mexican. They said I was stupid, and that I was "raggy" because I had just one outfit and the old, worn out shoes.

Their cruelty started slow. I remember the first day that many of the kids stood around after school and told me I smelled. I thought that it would not happen like that again, but it only got worse. They started to do this in the halls, at lunch, before classes, and at almost any time of the school day.

A Way Out

One day, one of the boys, Jon, was passing me in the hallway and hit me with his shoulder. It was so hard, and I did not expect it. I fell down on the floor. "Watch out, wetback!" he yelled. His friends laughed, and they walked away down the hall.

I picked up my papers, but some of the kids just walked on them. I was tugging some of the papers under a kid's foot when my hand slipped, and I got the worst paper cut ever. It burned, and I sucked my hand to try to slow down the gush of blood.

I finished picking up my papers and books and went to the bathroom to wash my hand. I don't know why I did it, but as I was washing it, I started to poke the cut with my fingernail. It hurt, but for some reason, feeling that pain felt nice.

The pain that came when I pushed my fingernail deeper into the cut was bigger than the voices of the kids running through my head. Instead of feeling all of the shame that their mean words caused, I felt just the pain of the cut on my hand. I don't know how to describe it any better than that, but it was something that let me feel, even for just a second, that I had escaped.

As I had walked into that bathroom, I had a thousand voices and images in my mind. All of those kids calling me names, making me feel ugly and horrible, Samuel sneaking into my bed, and the dirty clothes. All of it spun around in my brain all of the time.

When my fingernail went too deep into that cut, the pain it caused was like someone pushed the mute button on the remote control for our TV. Suddenly, everything was quiet, and the only thing in my head was the pain from the cut.

As you might guess, this was not a good solution to all of the pain I was feeling.

Chapter Three

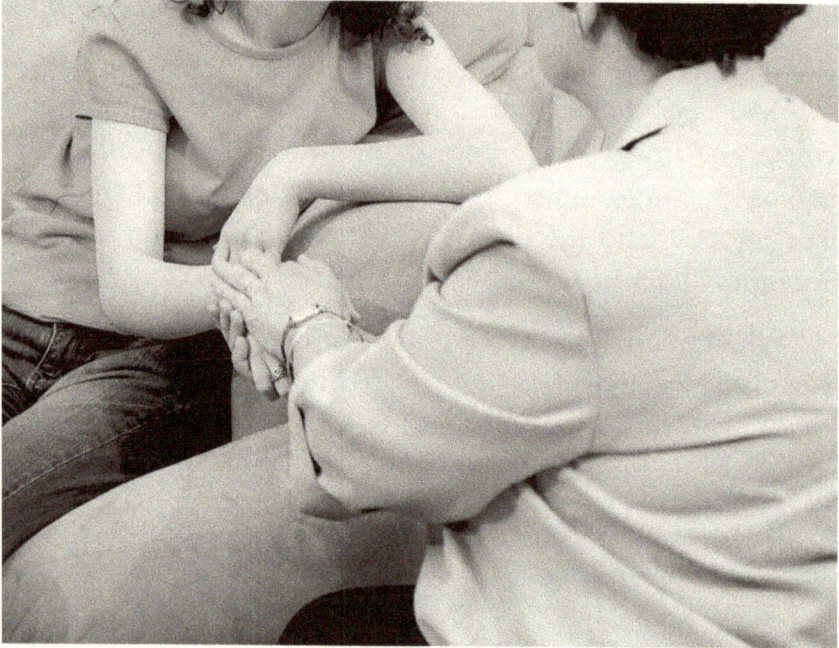

THE LOWEST TIME

That weird moment in the bathroom let me see that I didn't have to feel upset, confused or lost. I could just give myself some pain, and everything would get quiet. I wouldn't feel anything except the pain I was giving myself.

Finally, I could control something about my miserable life.

If I think about it now, I can see that I had no words to explain what was happening to me in my life. It was not because I was still just learning English or because I had no one to talk to (though I really believed there was no one to listen to me); it was just that everything was too much.

I was so alone, so sad, and I missed home and my family in a way that made me feel sick to think about. I could not picture my parents' faces without also feeling like I was torn in two. My heart was in Mexico, and the rest of me was here in this awful place where I was just a Mexican kid that no one wanted around.

And I was so tired. Sometimes I was too tired to even lift my head and look around. I was too tired to comb my hair, wash my face or body, or do anything. Sometimes I didn't even get out of my clothes at night.

At that moment, I felt that I was the most disgusting, ugly, and unwanted person on the planet. If I could make all of that stop by just cutting my arm or hand a bit, then it was the perfect solution.

IT BEGINS

After that day, I began to make frequent trips to the school bathroom, using my fingernails to slice into my skin whenever I felt that the other kids were getting to me.

The day the girl called me a pig in Spanish, and they chanted it at the table, or the day the nurse called me to her office and had the Spanish-speaking lady tell me that I had to do better about hygiene… All of these things ended with me making a trip to the bathroom to cut myself and enjoy some relief.

At home, the cutting was also my way of soothing myself. Whenever things got too noisy, crowded, and crazy, I would hide somewhere and cut myself. I tried always to keep my cuts in places you couldn't see, but sometimes they were on my arms and legs too.

Fortunately, the nighttime visits to my bed stopped when Samuel learned that I was bleeding. He understood that I might become pregnant, and so it made him leave me alone. Knowing that he was waiting for another young girl to arrive also made me feel guilty and horrible because I thought it was my fault he would start in on her too.

So, even though I was free of his torment, I was still thinking about him because he was just waiting for the next victim, and I could not do anything to stop it.

Whenever I was upset by such things, I turned to cutting. Cutting was my great release for everything, but you might not know that cutters have to keep making bigger or deeper cuts if they want the same results.

CUTTING AND BULLYING

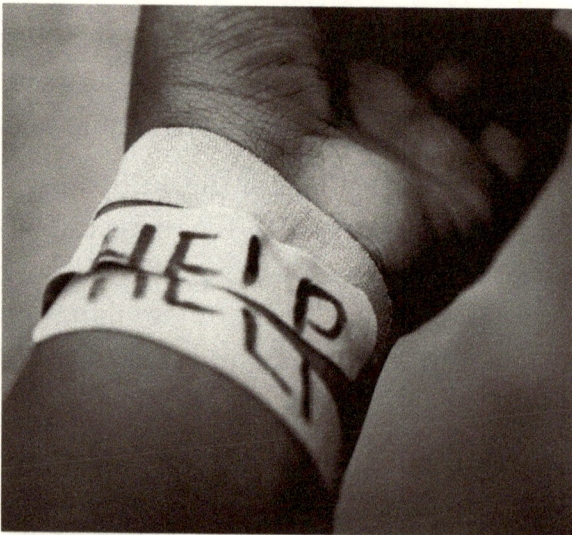

Sara, a girl I met much later, and who was also a cutter, said that she decided to ask for help when she realized that it was always going to take more pain to give her those few minutes of peace.

"I just knew that I would have to start making really huge cuts and that these would be hard to hide," she said to me one day. "I asked for help to stop myself from doing a lot more harm to my body... I was seriously afraid that I might accidentally kill myself."

Unfortunately, I was not in the same place in my life. I did not know that I had anyone to turn to for help. So, I kept making my cuts larger, deeper, and more severe. Instead of my fingernail, I was using pencils to dig deep gouges into my skin, and even these were not making me feel better.

I tried to hide my cuts, and yet even when they were seen, no one at my house seemed to notice. Wearing an old t-shirt that someone in the house gave me, it was easy to see my scars all over the place. The huge scars along with new and fresh wounds looked scary in the mirror, and yet no one at home said a word.

At school, kids called me a freak and made fun of me for the marks on my arms. "Do you enjoy picking all of your scabs?" one of the meaner girls asked. "If you want to die so badly," she went on, "you should just kill yourself."

When she said that, I realized that suicide had never occurred to me. I had not thought about ending my life. From that day on, though, I began to wonder about it.

"If the cutting stops taking away the pain," I thought to myself, "then I'll do it."

Until then, the cutting had still worked, but I needed to go deeper and bigger. I did wonder if I might accidentally kill myself. The cuts were getting more severe and some took a long time to stop bleeding. I also had some older cuts that looked infected, and I began to feel a dark and deep despair that I was never going to escape my misery.

I actually felt even more depressed at the thought that my cutting was not going to work. Sometimes, I would do it, and I would feel like I was free of my body. Even though it was just a few minutes, I felt totally free. So, I actually felt very sad that I might lose that feeling.

"The cutting is not even keeping me happy anymore," I began to realize. And it happened even as the kids around me began to tease me more. I just became more and more sad and lost, "I should probably end my life...why am I scared of just ending it?" I remember saying aloud to myself one day.

Now I know that if I had been in a healthy home and with my family, things would never have gone so far. Maybe, things like this would have never even started. However, I was a teenage girl who had gone through puberty without anyone to talk to about it or to answer my questions. I had been sexually abused by a man in my home, and he still lived there, though he did not come to my bed any longer. I was very poor and without any money to buy newer clothes to stop kids from teasing me, and I also had trouble keeping up with hygiene. I was a Mexican immigrant and treated like dirt because of it - even though I had survived a hard journey across the desert to make it here.

My self-esteem did not exist. I truly believed I had no hope of ever living a normal and happy life again. I did not fit in the foreign land where I was living, and I was so lost that I just wanted to escape.

I thought my chance to escape had finally arrived one day when the worst of my bullies did something horrible.

Chapter Four

THE WORST AND BEST DAYS

On my worst day ever, the biggest and dumbest of my many bullies, Adam, decided to torment me at lunch. I was sitting alone, as usual, and it no longer bothered me. That day, I was actually feeling a tiny bit happy because I had been able to earn some money babysitting one of the kids in the house. His mother gave me a few dollars for watching him, and after a few weeks, I had enough to go to the thrift shop and buy a few new clothes.

I had picked out a new pair of jeans and a few new shirts. I was wearing my favorite shirt. It was pale blue with stripes, and I loved it. I loved the way it smelled, the way it felt, and the way it looked with my hair and skin. I felt pretty for once, and so what happened next was a disaster.

My bully had a habit of picking on me at lunch. One day he spit on my food. Another day he took something right from my plate. Once, he even took something out of my hand as I was putting it towards my mouth.

"Please..." he sneered at me one day, "Uh...I mean, por favor," he laughed, and his friends laughed too, "Can you just stop eating those disgusting Mexican foods? You already smell like a fart, and now you smell even worse than one!" he said looking into my eyes.

"That food is disgusting," one of his friends said over his shoulder, "Almost as disgusting as you."

They had no idea what I ate or what it smelled like because they were never close enough to see or tell, but they liked to pick on me.

On my worst day, Adam took the cheap juice box in my lunch and picked it up. He pretended to look at it, and nodding his head he said, "Good, that should get you clean." He then sprayed the juice through the straw onto my face and shirt.

The liquid was bright red, so I knew it was never coming out of the shirt. I couldn't believe he had done that. I was so used to him just picking something up and walking away; I was sure he was going to take the juice box and keep on walking.

As I wiped at my eyes, he laughed and said, "You should shower more."

After that, he walked away and didn't look back. I just stared at him for a few minutes. I was thinking a thousand things.

I wanted to scream and swear at him in English and Spanish, and then I looked down at my lovely new shirt that was now all spotted with bright red dots of juice. For some reason, the shirt getting ruined felt like someone had just stomped on my heart.

I went to the bathroom to try to clean it up, and I could see that it was not going to come out. My new shirt, the one that I loved, and I didn't even get to wear it for a day. That bully had no idea that he had just ruined something that took me weeks to save for, and he had laughed at me when he did it.

I went into the stall with a pencil and started to stick it against my arm. I heard the door open and some girls came in, so I waited. I just breathed in and out, waiting for them to go. As I did, I looked up at the bar over the door of the bathroom stall, and I realized that I couldn't endure anymore.

"The cutting isn't the escape for you," I remember saying to myself. "You need to get away from all of this really…just get away…"

I was so full of bad feelings, and nothing was going to free me of them.

"You go to bed miserable. You wake up miserable, and spend your days miserable…and for what?" I began to cry as I mumbled to myself, "All of my dreams are gone. I can't even remember what kinds of dreams I had!"

I kept on going, telling myself what I needed to hear to take the steps I thought would release me from the pain, "You are lower than the dirt on the ground…"

There was still something inside of me arguing against what I was thinking. I remember telling myself that I had been through more, seen more, and felt more than the kids who were teasing and bullying me each day, and none of them could see that. Maybe if they could see that? I had a glimmer of hope, and then the misery came back loud and clear.

"See you?" my thoughts seemed to remind me, "At home, you are invisible, and no one wants you to make any sort of trouble, even if you are being hurt!"

"Just do it," my mind kept repeating, "There is nothing good about life, and it is better if you just end it all."

The two girls had left the bathroom, and so I took off my beautiful new shirt, tied it over the bar above the stall door, and made a tight loop out of the sleeve and part of the shirt. I slipped the loop over my head and let my feet slide from under me.

I could feel the immense pressure of my blood stuck in my head; I could see spots in front of my eyes and hear the pounding in my ears. I knew I was going to black out, and for one second I asked myself if this was what I wanted…

"Do you really want to die?" I remember thinking, and then I felt panic, but I was so dizzy that I could not even move or lift up my arms…and then it all went dark…

BEGINNING AGAIN

I woke up in a bright room. It was not sunlight; it was electric lights, and the room was very bare. I wondered if this was, somehow, heaven. Then I heard voices and saw people moving past the door. I tried to sit up, but I was secured to my bed. I realized that my hands and my feet were tied.

Suddenly, it all came back to me. The juice all over my shirt, the rush to the bathroom, and the choice to end my life. And even this had failed.

What I learned from my social worker, Anne-Marie, later that day was that a teacher had come in just as I had blacked out. She saw my feet under the stall and realized what I had done. She called for help and lifted me up from the floor to take all of the weight off my neck. She had saved my life.

An ambulance came and took me to the hospital to be sure that I was okay.

"You're lucky to be alive," she said, "Just a moment or two more and you would not have been okay."

They didn't see that I didn't care at all about any of it. I had wanted to die. When I opened my eyes and realized that I was in the hospital, I wanted to die even more.

NEW SURROUNDINGS

People tell me all kinds of things, and one of the things that I learned in the hospital was a saying about dark clouds having silver linings. What they meant was that even a dark storm cloud has the sun behind it, and that something good is always there - even if we can't see it right away.

"The trip to the hospital," Anne-Marie said, "is a bit of good luck."

"Why?" I asked her, feeling more miserable than ever.

"Well," she said, "You're alive, and you now have go to a mental health hospital for a while, to recover."

I must have looked scared at that, and so she held my hand and said, "People, especially teens, who try to kill themselves always have to have a recovery period."

How will that help me? I thought.

I quickly discovered that it was a time that probably helped to save me. As funny as it sounds, my time at the mental health hospital was one of the best times.

At the hospital, I had clean bedding, clean clothes, food, daily showers, and people who wanted to talk with me about all that I was feeling and experiencing. Even though my English was still not the best, they wanted me to tell them everything that I could.

I am not going to lie - as good as it was for me to talk, it was still so hard to tell strangers just what I had been through, what I was thinking, and how I felt.

LOOKING ACROSS THE BORDER

Angela, one of my therapists, told me that it is always easier if we just start at the beginning.

"Look back as far as you can," she said, "And just tell me the things you can see in your mind."

So I did, and I told her everything that I could remember. I told her about Mexico, my parents, grandparents, and my two sisters. I told her about the poverty that kept us so low and how we all wished we could have something better for ourselves. I told her about the dreams we had of life in America where we could work, get good food, find a nice home, and feel safer than we could ever feel in Mexico. I talked about our plans to pay to get me across the border and how I would work and become the hero of the story, making a path for my family to follow.

I began to cry when talking about all of my dreams. "None of my dreams will ever come true now," I sobbed, "At least not in the ways I hoped."

Right then, I started to see that I began sinking into what was called "depression" when things started to go so wrong.

"I got to America," I went on, "And everything was horrible...not one truly nice or happy thing has ever happened here."

Then I started to talk about the way life really was for me in America. Samuel's visits to my bed, puberty, the miserable teasing and bullying at school, the terrible poverty, and my discovery of cutting.

"I could never fit in," I explained "And that caused a lot of pain. I was so alone in the world, and not even the other kids in my school would let me in or make friends with me."

"How did that make you feel?" Angela gently asked.

"Like I shouldn't even be alive," I said honestly, "And when everything was spinning and screaming in my head, the pain of cutting took it all away."

I showed her my arms and my legs, and I told her how I went from using my fingernails to make light cuts to digging into my arms and legs with a pencil tip.

"I saw that it started to take more and more pain," I said with a bit of shame, "It was the only way to free myself from the emotional pain I had to live with all of the time."

It felt so good to let it all come pouring out, and it was the first time I had a chance to take a good look at myself. I did not see how much pain I was in, and that I had allowed it to swallow me up. I did not realize how lost I was.

It didn't all come out at once, at least not clearly. The therapist saw me many times, and each time I told her more and more of the story or gave her answers to questions about things we had talked about.

REALIZATION

Doing this therapy made me see a few things about myself that I had not realized before. For one thing, I was the brave girl my Mama had said I could be. I had made the journey, survived it, lived through serious challenges, and was still trying to regain my hope.

"That," my therapist said, "is a true sign of bravery."

I also realized that I was strong. Because I had lived through the worst of times, I was a pretty tough girl.

And I finally saw just how smart I was.

"It takes a lot to see past the trouble, the pain, the confusion, and all of the rest," Angela reminded me. "You were able to look at it all, without trying to run away and hide from it, and when you did that, you have become much more able to understand yourself better."

She was right. "It was fear and isolation that made me do some things," I said during one of our meetings, "and it was courage and willpower to do others."

I could see myself without trying to explain away things or to make excuses. Angela kept reminding me that this showed my intelligence.

"It's called emotional intelligence," she said, "And it is going to end up being something that you treasure throughout life."

We also started to work on things known as "triggers". These were things that caused me to cut myself and think about escaping.

"You have been through so much," she said, "It may be hard for us to figure out just what causes you to feel like you must escape, but it is important that we do."

We spent a lot of time talking about the things that made me feel most like running away. The boy ruining my shirt was something we started with. It was not that he embarrassed me in front of my classmates. It was not that he took my juice. It was that he took something that gave me self-esteem.

"You need to rebuild your self-esteem," Angela said many times, "And to do that, you need more than just me and you talking about it."

This was why she was working with others to help me find people who understood my particular situation.

Chapter Five

A NEW JOURNEY

As I spent time getting better and getting to know myself more, I learned some important facts.

"A lot of people who are immigrants into another country might face racism or discrimination," Angela explained, "That boy who picked on you for your Mexican food targeted your self-esteem."

"When he told me I stank because I was Mexican, and all of the other mean things," I asked, "That is what knocked down my self-esteem?"

"Sure," Angela said, "It attacked the thing you missed the most - your home, and made it into something smelly, dirty, unwanted, and bad."

I had not realized that the dislike that people showed me as an immigrant was also a huge part of the trouble and pain I carried.

With Angela's help, I also realized that the people I was living with were not helping me, either. Yes, they were also immigrants from the same country, but as she said, "You lived in a place where it was everyone for themselves. No one paid attention, and no one cared."

Even though I felt bad about people making fun of me for being "Mexican," I was surrounded by fellow Mexicans who were not showing me that all of the bad things being said were wrong. There were people who smelled, who were nasty and mean, and who were not good people at all.

"You need a family," Angela said with a tiny grin, "What you need the most is to be with individuals who understood what it was like to be an immigrant all alone."

I thought about that for a while, and at first, I didn't like it. After all, I had Mama, Papa, and my sisters, and I said that to Angela.

"I know," she said, "But right now you need a new family that can start to fill up the emptiness that was left when you came across the border. But," she added, "It needs to be a family that really understands you…who helps you to stop feeling isolated." isolation.

And it was here that my luck changed, and my experience in America began to be one that was about brightness, hope, and happier days.

NO LONGER ALONE

After I had gone to the hospital, it was impossible to be ignored. I had a green card, and the people at the house had been responsible for sponsoring me, but they were not my family, and they were not taking care of me.

"They are neglecting and mistreating you," Angela said, "They cannot give you the care or supervision you need. So, you are going to get the same attention that all abused kids receive. The first step is getting a foster home."

This sounds scary when you are being told about it, and you will hear a lot of bad things. I heard a lot of bad things.

"I've gone from home to home," said Jeremy (one of the boys I met while at the mental hospital), "Some of them are okay, and some are very bad."

"How can you be sure it is going to be okay?" I asked Angela.

"Don't worry," she reassured me, "I am going to keep an eye on you and your situation…it will work out fine!"

The first foster home was kind of bad, and I worried that Jeremy was right - it was never going to be a good place to live. The house was crowded. The food was terrible, and it was always noisy and busy. Things were dirty, and I think the people who were my foster parents should have said no to taking on so many kids, but I believe that they wanted the money too.

No one was mean to me, but when I started at a new school and struggled with being alone and with fears of bullying, I thought about cutting again. This time, I understood that I was becoming depressed, and I told my social worker right away. She came for a visit, saw how crowded and hectic it was, and she said that she was going to see if I could be located to a different place.

I went to bed that night feeling sad. Here I was, all alone again, being tossed around from place to place.

Will I to go to another school? I worried, *What if the next place is worse? What if I'm such a problem that they just ignore me?*

I was afraid to speak out again, and I was too scared to do much of anything. After just a few days, one of my foster parents said that I had to move to a new place and that I would leave at dinner time that night. I could tell they were angry or annoyed about it, and when I left they hardly said goodbye.

"Okay," Angela said with a big smile, "I know that was not so great, but I think you'll really like the next one."

"I hope so too," was all I could say.

I worried that I had made a big mistake. Then we pulled up to a beautiful house on a quiet street. The house had a small yard with a birdfeeder hanging from a post. There were a few flowers and some pots of plants on the front porch.

It was clean and quiet, and I thought that we were at the wrong place. Angela rang the bell, and a friendly little boy answered the door. With his brown skin and big, dark eyes I thought he might be from Mexico too.

"David!" he shouted without turning from the door. His eyes were so sweet, and he reminded me of one of my little cousins at home.

He yelled again, and soon a smiling man came down the stairs with a young girl on his hip.

I was introduced to David (my foster Dad), his wife Terry (my foster Mom), and the three other kids in the house. One of them was just three; her name was Sarah. The little boy at the door was actually from Guatemala, and he was Adrian. There was another boy who was around ten, and he was from Mexico. His name was Nelson. I would be the older sister again!

They took me around the house and showed me the room that would be mine. Angela stayed for a while, and then said, "Okay, Flora...I have to go."

She looked down into my face, "I think it is going to be just fine." I shook my head yes because I felt at home already.

I thought I was dreaming. A room to myself! Clean places to eat, play, and a bathroom just for the four kids!

Of course, it wasn't perfect. Nelson had a lot of problems. He had learning disabilities. He also had seizures and needed medicine, and he could act up when we were in public places, but we all learned how to help him and our foster parents. It was crazy sometimes because we had to get to work and school, and I had homework and struggled with English.

But it all felt right. At last, I was going to be able to learn and to get healthy and happy, and I could start thinking about my dreams again.

"You are rebuilding yourself, Flora," Terry would say, "You have been through so much, so you should just start again and be a kid again!"

It was so nice having someone to talk to, especially because David and Terry both spoke Spanish. I didn't have to struggle to find words, and I started to feel like myself, my real self.

FEELING BETTER

I bet you wonder if I feel all better, and if I ever think about cutting or even killing myself anymore? I will be honest and say that I don't feel all better. I feel like I am healing and that I have seen more than anyone my age should see.

At my group therapy one day, I admitted it, "I feel lucky because I learned so much from all of my struggles and found a real home," I said, "But I still miss my family."

I often wonder if this life with my foster family is the only family life I will have again. My parents still cannot afford to come to America, and though I can now write to them, they say that the money is just too hard to save. It is so hard to understand that I live in a nice place, with good people, and feel happy and safe, but my family does not.

So, I cannot truly feel better because I will always want to go home to my parents. I know it sounds terrible to say that because of how great my foster family is, but it is true. Still, I always feel like a big piece of me is missing and still back across the border in Mexico.

I can't focus on that, though. If I have learned anything from the therapists and counselors, and the many friends I talk to when I go to some of my therapy meetings, it is that I have to focus on the positive…always.

One counselor always reminds us, "When you are depressed, it is too easy to think only about the negative. That got some of you into trouble in the past, and so now you need to look at the good things."

WHEN YOU ARE DEPRESSED

"My name is Flora, and I am a teenage girl from Mexico," I said at my latest therapy session with other kids, "I left my family behind to come to America and try to make a path for the rest of them to follow me. It did not work out that way."

"Instead, I ended up isolated and alone among people who did not take care of me. I was a kid in a foreign country. I couldn't speak English. I didn't have money, and I did not know a lot about the world. I was abused in many ways, bullied and tormented at school, and I was in such deep emotional pain that I started harming myself. Things spun so out of control that I tried to kill myself. It was then, when I had done more than cried out for help but had actually given up, that I got help."

Because it was a group session for teens who had attempted suicide, my counselor told me I should share the whole story, or as much as I was comfortable sharing. So, I decided to admit to feeling ashamed.

"I do not like telling people my story because I still feel sad, ashamed, and even angry about it," I said, "But I am sharing it with you because I want you to see that being depressed is a bit like being outside of yourself and far away from reality."

"That's right, Flora," our counselor added, "When you are depressed, it happens for many reasons. People might not have suffered the ways that you did. Their life might not have been as challenging, and yet they still feel very depressed or sad. It is okay - it is not bad or weird to be depressed. It is not something you can control."

"She is right. There is so little that we can control and so many things can make you depressed:"

"Maybe you are lonely as I was, and kids at school only make it worse?

Maybe someone hurt you, and you feel scared to tell anyone, and that makes you feel isolated and alone?

Maybe you just feel sad, and it won't go away?

What I have learned from others is that you can be depressed and not understand what is happening or why. It is not your fault. You did not do anything to cause it. The good news is that you can do things to start feeling better.

Look at me - as soon as I started to tell someone about myself, I felt amazing. I could not stop talking, thinking about what I wanted to share with my therapist, and the words just poured out. I did not even ask for any answers or solutions to my problems, I just needed to share them with someone.

It was only after I had said all of the things I needed to say that I started to want help. I had let it all out, and because of that, I was able to feel like myself again and feel like I wanted to get better. It was only then that I even believed that things could get better.

If I had a friend and was not so alone, I probably would have told them everything all along. Perhaps that friend could have helped me to keep my self-esteem and my confidence - even if things were not so good after coming to America. The problem was that I was isolated and after a while, I wanted to just stay isolated."

That is a big mistake when you are depressed.

"Being alone only makes things worse," Angela said when we first met after I said I just wanted everyone to go away and leave me alone. "It is important to find at least one friend or person to talk to," she continued, "And not only online. You must find a real-world friend and sit down together to talk."

My foster parents are now the people I can talk to easiest, and they are helping and taking good care of me. They understand what I went through, and together we make sure that anything that triggers my depression is kept under control. We also do a lot of things together like yard work, cooking meals, playing games, and going for walks.

I learned that just doing exercise, like running with the kids, riding my bike, and going swimming, is a great way to stop myself from feeling sad or upset. I am even teaching the other kids how to do some folk dancing that my mother taught me!

Today I understand that anyone can be depressed because anyone can feel alone, sad, isolated, and lost. Sometimes it can even be as bad as what I had to go through, and some kids aren't as lucky as me. I was lucky. My teacher found me and saved my life. The people at the hospital kept me going and helped to show me that I wasn't alone. My foster parents have become my new family, and yet they know how sad I am all of the time about my parents and sisters in Mexico.

Like I said at the beginning of this book, I left a big piece of myself back across the border, and I think I took a big piece of my parents and sisters with me too. Sometimes I try to think of it like that - they are with me, and I am with them. Sometimes it is too hard to think about them.

I know that it is easy to let depression take hold of you and drag you away from life. I was lucky, and I was able to fight back. You can too. I hope you learned from my story and that you know that you are never alone. There is always someone who wants to help you…you just have to ask. I did, and I am here today because of it.

Sources

ACF.HHS.gov. Foster Care.
http://www.acf.hhs.gov/programs/cb/focus-areas/foster-care

HelpGuide.org. Teenager's Guide to Depression.
http://www.helpguide.org/articles/depression/teenagers-guide-to-depression.htm

KidsHealth.org. TeensHealth: Depresssion.
http://kidshealth.org/teen/your_mind/mental_health/depression.html

Other Books by Patrice M Foster

1. A guide to teenage depression
2. Left across the Border series 1
3. Tainted by Hate Series 3
4. The Journey Home A memoir